This Time
of Life

Contents

I met Mary Kellogg a decade ago. I loved and admired her from the first time I saw her. She was just the kind of woman I wanted to be. Independent, honest, loving and creative.

When Jon and I first read the poems, she reluctantly showed us, we both looked at each other and said, people need to see these. We have to publish them.

We are proud to publish Mary's fourth book "This Time Of Life" with love and admiration.

Maria Wulf

Silence in Life

older age, no one knows
because it is within me
not an easy thing

sitting on a life line shelf
a not so funny place to be
this really should not bother you

you know you could do all of that
but hands and body do not want to stretch
this leaves more time to do what you want to do

chair to sit on to weed the garden, lawn mower with
comfortable seat to ride, watch the grand kids and
the birds as you fill their feeder

we get stuck on past time memories the joys
and times we had. this makes us sad. So change direction
put some new lights on this stage of life. Do for others
that are lacking. Be happy that this gift is given. Listen and
    love this
time of life.

September 19, 2017

The Meadow Beyond

I stand awe struck in the grasp of beauty
As a flow of air rises gently caressing my soul
I hear its coming
pulling tips of meadow grass in its wake
searching knowing light years beyond
does it begin again on a towering mountain
opening slots of freedom
as it ruffles spice of meadow
to stretch out minds of knowing

June 14, 2017

Moonlight Listening Secrets

full moon light
shuffles across the lawn with
mysterious purpose
beyond my yard and room

venturing out in bare feet
path cool and damp
trees draft hard shadows
I listen as voices seep
from the long porch

hide by the raspberries
stifle my giggle
knowing it is forbidden
they do not want me here
listening.

April 2010

Mother Never Wore Slacks

off to church or into the hen house
mother wore cotton dresses
stockings of cotton
always a plain tan color
under all the harness of girdle
I don't know whether she needed it or not
as she was not rotund but very well shaped and solid.

her pleasant face round and hopeful
no enemies in her life
she saw life and took life straight ahead
she lived in that challenge
Mom did what she felt was hers to do

She had great energy. She was strong.
She would march off to the blueberry field alone
come home and make a pie for supper.

She could have a jolly good laugh
laugh until tears rolled down her round face.

her once blond hair now dark speckled with white
fell to her waist when undone.
bound tightly in a bun for chores.

she was fast at figuring people and could spot a phony
    in a first visit.
She was friendly to many that were not welcomed by
    all persons. Lesbian neighbors or

castoffs like lonesome widows and an elderly lady barroom
   owner broken and ill, that
others shunned.

Her faith was her deep strength as she plowed through
   her life. She was very honest sometimes blunt in her
   opinions. She would give people names that fit the
   character. One such was Scrooge. A miserly man they
   rented from one time. She would say he was counting his
   money in his gold room. Another comment on a not so
   strong husband, the wife makes the snow balls and he has
   to throw them.

raking the chicken shit off the boards in the hen house
sometimes on a Sunday as the hired help were not there
Aunt Lil tutting around the kitchen. "she shouldn't do
   that!"
Mom did what she felt was hers to do. She had great
   energy. She was strong.

June 25, 2012

Bluebird

bluebird call is softly spoken
    pleading in love and rescue

flight a gentle floating feather
    kissing the world

April 2010

Sounds of Winter

I ski deep in the woods
slicing a track thru new snow

lofty hemlocks shake their shoulders
to sprinkle snow powder

errant ice crystals play in the air
celebrating a lone woodpecker's tapping

distant trees knock in the crackling cold
rubbing the skins of their neighbors

this muffled cloak envelopes me
with sumptuous sounds of winter.

November 2008

The Photo

Seeing you
hair tossed by a sea spray breeze
my hand in yours and you kneeling
braced against the little beached skiff
the photo drove me deep within myself

you smiling
so full of life and expectant curious visage

years will pass
and times of walking on the beach
hand in hand with
our young minds
thoughts inside pristine

now with aching heart
I long to hold that hand
kiss that mouth love that body as onc

every day was a new one
did we notice it?
full of plans, worries, saving for this and that
trips to spirit filled mountain tops

where have moments gone
moments that filled every minute
important moments
some held
some forgotten beyond my reach.

Today the sun is warm
bright and loving. I look up and realize the stars are still
    there.
set in the abyss of blue.
A favorite hymn. God gives Freely accept Freely.
A fair exchange.

February 22, 2010

Quandry

Mallard Duck's Search is on
Mallard ducks appear on my quiet frog pond
Male resplendent with emerald cap

Forceful female checks the area
"no place for my house on these slate step beds
No place for laundry out to dry
grass too short to hide my nest

decides: we must go back to the big pond
seek new choice
father says "just look a bit, please"
Mary likes to watch us"
sorry we're moving on up the hill to nest
with the loud friendly geese

September 2017

Remembering

One little girl was lonesome sometimes
I did not realize in myself that was true

I made up my own friends, Nancy and Sue
hidden just for me
in my club behind the ice house
Ours a small ring of stones

summer days would pass with play
pretend school and doll time dressing

till sister calls to collect chicken's eggs
a fun time challenge
with hope they were not nesting

September 2017

Isolation

wind sucks breath of life
in relentless grasp of land
poking nose into cracks and crevices
seeking to chill beyond borders

snow ferrets its way to hiss in the hearth
seeking steam from the warming fire
fingers of warmth dance and ignore the interruption

smallest of little creatures
exiled to beat a path beneath the snow
search warm tunnels
for cache of seeds

barnyard dwellers
press backs to the storm
muster strength
to defeat the stinging whip of ice

screen of white
erases pines and meadow

Isolation fills the void.

September 2009

Humming Birds At My Feeder

Big fellow with a fancy shine

waits to clear his destination

swings to chase away intruders
flipping back and forth

his command of the whole area

"it is mine he shows
    it is mine"

September 2017

Fluffy Stuff

the bristles of the mushroom shaped brush
collect a gob of white fluff
tight lipped Dad spreads the mix
on his facial plain
finishing with a flourish
he sets a fluff marshmallow
on my nose

January 8, 2010

Spring Bulbs Transplant

core is already thrusting forth
in search of sun and air
to breath in wash of rain

I dig the bulb
its pregnant body
cool and moist in my hand

April 2010

Comfort Care

we accept death in the far distance future
one small thing that humans think about
large within heart and soul

observe the mirror in a drop of rain
reflection around the orb
small things of life
make all of life an epic of feelings
fears, plans, future, love, forgiveness

as the shadows lengthen
destiny with comfort and care
softens transition whether within
few minutes, hours or days to see, hear
love, laugh, live this final passage of time
gentle hands to hold
pateience to listen
love to give
comfort care

December 2011

Rolling Down Hill

a soft grassy knoll
beckons
down we lie
set to travel, to roll
spinning
grass, dirt, sky
content
dizzying
grass, dirt, sky
content

April 2010

Mary Kellogg is a poet and nature lover. This is her fourth volume of poetry. She lives in the Holcomb Adult Care Facility in Granville, NY.

May 10, 2006

177 South Grimes Hill Rd.
Granville, N.Y. 12832

Dear Mr. Katz,

I live in Hebron on So. Grimes Hill, just east over a few hills
from Patterson Hill.

In June I will have four visitors, lady friends from 40 plus
years ago when we all lived in the Katonah, NY area.

All are dog lovers, some widowed(as I), great grandmothers and
grandmothers still interested in many learniig experiences.

I was wondering if we might visit your farm for a short time
one day in June. They will be here on the 13th and 14th.

We all have enjoyed your books. We are a quiet group!

Thank you for considering my request.

Yours truly,

Mary Kellogg